For Cole.
May this story always remind you of the impact
one small, loving gesture can have.
—*LM*

For my father, who has always loved Bears.
—*SB*

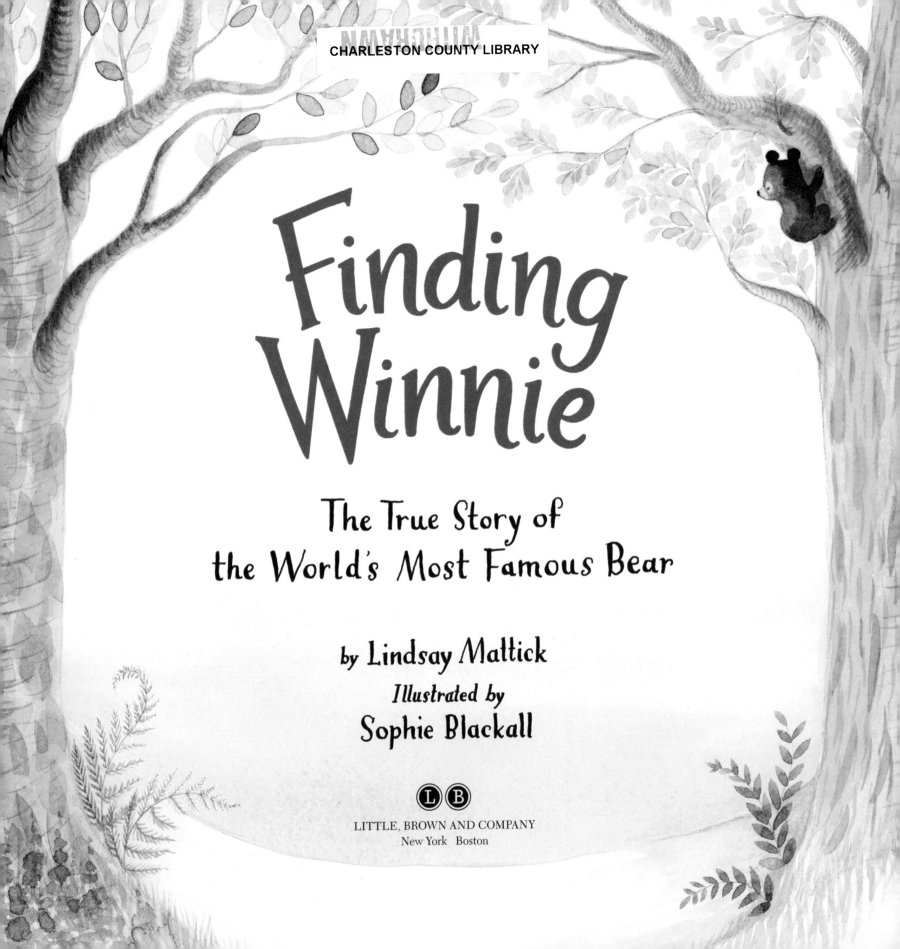

Finding Winnie

The True Story of the World's Most Famous Bear

by Lindsay Mattick

Illustrated by
Sophie Blackall

(L)(B)
LITTLE, BROWN AND COMPANY
New York Boston

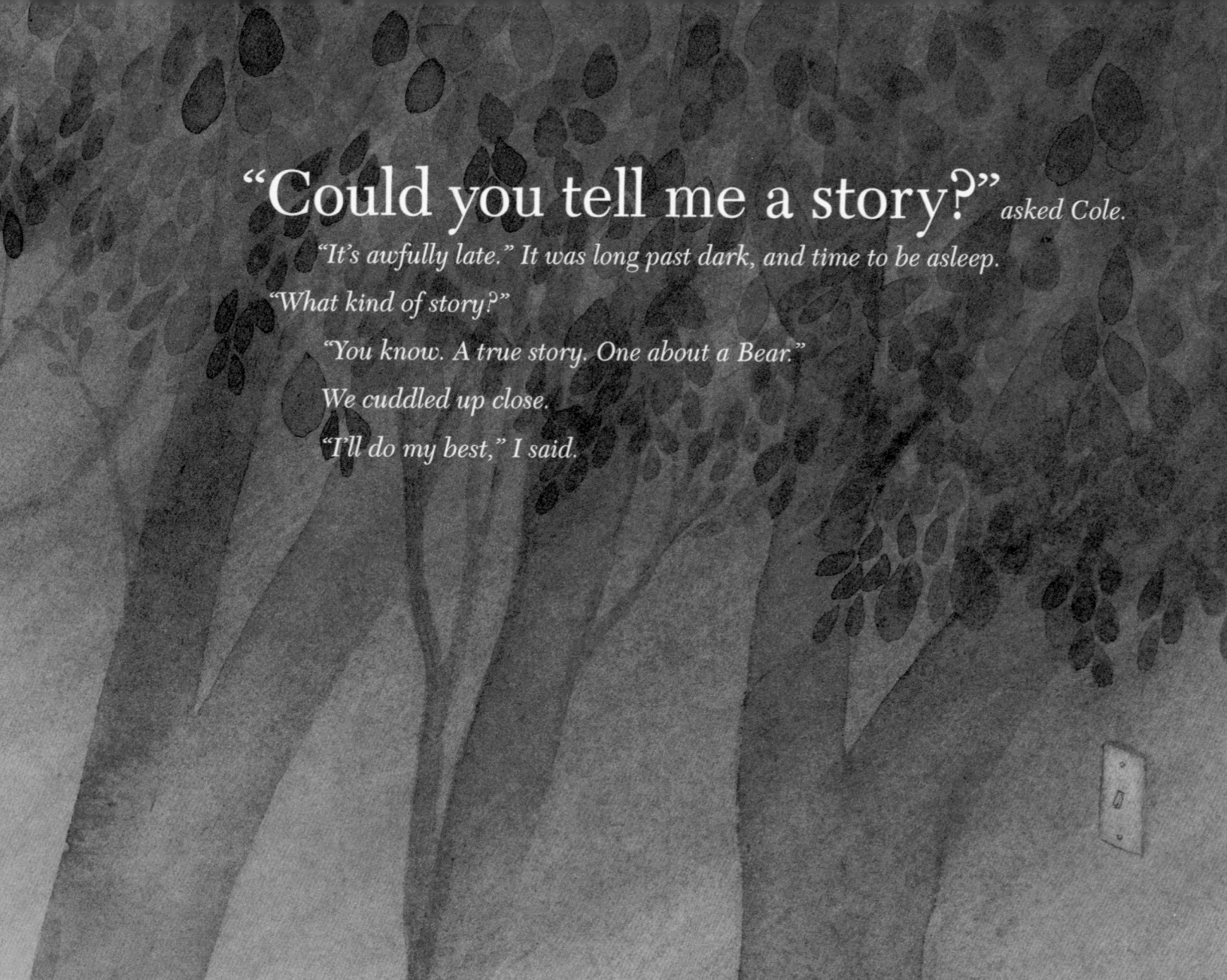

"Could you tell me a story?" *asked Cole.*

"It's awfully late." It was long past dark, and time to be asleep.

"What kind of story?"

"You know. A true story. One about a Bear."

We cuddled up close.

"I'll do my best," I said.

A very long time ago,

about a hundred years before you were
born, there was a veterinarian who lived in
Winnipeg. His name was Harry Colebourn.

"A vegetarian?" said Cole. "Bear doesn't
like vegetables."

"A veterinarian. It means an animal
doctor."

"I know that!" Cole said. "That's what
I'm going to maybe be when I'm big."

If a horse had the hiccups or a cow had
a cough, Harry knew how to make them
feel just right. Harry's hands were never
cold, even in Winnipeg, where winters
are so frosty that icicles grow on the insides
of your nose. That was just the kind of
doctor he was.

But a day came when Harry had to say good-bye to Winnipeg. There was a war far, far away—beyond the end of the country and on the other side of the ocean—and he was going to help. He would be caring for the soldiers' horses.

Harry rode east on a train full of other soldiers. He leaned his head against the window, watching the land scroll by, wondering what it would be like to be so far from home.

The train rolled right through dinner and over the sunset and around ten o'clock and
into a nap and out the next day, until it stopped at a place called White River.

Harry decided to stretch his legs.

On the train platform was a man on a bench with a baby.

"A baby?" said Cole, annoyed.

A baby bear. *A cub.*

Harry stopped. It's not every day
that you see a bear cub at a train station.
"That Bear has lost its mother," he
thought, "and that man must be the
trapper who got her."

"What do trappers do?" asked Cole.
"It's what trappers don't do. They
don't raise bears."
"Raise them?"
"You know," I said. "Love them."

Harry thought for a long time. Then he said to himself, "There *is* something special about that Bear." He felt inside his pocket and said, "I shouldn't." He paced back and forth and said, "I can't." Then his heart made up his mind, and he walked up to the trapper and said, "I'll give you twenty dollars for the bear."

"*Is twenty dollars a lot?*" asked Cole.
"*Back then?*" I said. "*Even more than a lot.*"

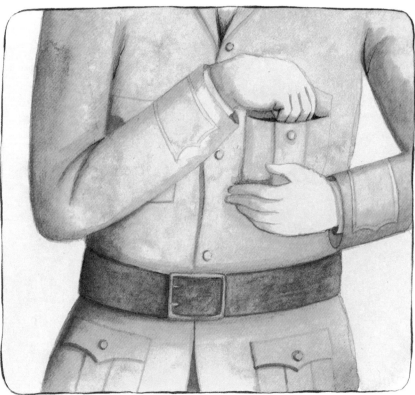

"Captain Colebourn!" said the Colonel on the train, as the little Bear sniffed at his knees. "We are on a journey of thousands of miles, heading into the thick of battle, and you propose to bring this Most Dangerous Creature?"

Bear stood straight up on her hind legs as if to salute the Colonel. The Colonel stopped speaking at once—and then, in quite a different voice, he said, "Oh, hallo."

The men of Harry's regiment squeezed by to have a look.

"I've decided to name her Winnipeg," Harry told them, "so we'll never be far from home. Winnie, for short."

They had a very long way to travel, and they had already gone three or four feet when Winnie grew hungry.

"What do bears eat?" the men wondered.

"What *don't* they eat?" said Harry.

"Vegetables!" Cole reminded me.

"Winnie ate vegetables," I said. "She ate everything, except onions."

They brought her carrots and potatoes, and apples and tomatoes, and eggs and beans and bread. And a tin of fish, and some slop in a dish. But Winnie was still hungry.

"How about dessert?" said Harry, holding up a bottle of condensed milk. Taking the treat in her paws, Winnie lay on her back and hummed a happy song as she drank. The men roared.

Harry and Winnie gathered with soldiers from all over Canada in the green fields of Valcartier.

A whole city of tents had sprung up there. One was a hospital for horses, where Harry went to work.

Winnie was in the army now. Harry taught her to stand up straight and hold her head high and turn this way and that, just so! Soon, she was assigned her own post.

Even the Colonel agreed that Winnie was a Remarkable Bear. She might have been the best navigator in the whole army. If you hid something, could she find it? She could! What if it was farther away? And farther still? "Remarkable!" he cried.

In the evenings, both of them were too tired to move.

When Harry thought about Winnie and the voyage across the ocean, his head said, "I shouldn't." His head said, "I can't." But his heart made up his mind.

Nobody had ever tried to float so many people and animals across the Atlantic Ocean before. Thirty ships sailed together, carrying about 36,000 men, and about 7,500 horses...and about one bear named Winnie.

When they finally arrived in England, the regiment went to training on the Salisbury Plain, where it rained and rained and rained.

But Winnie didn't seem to mind. She was the Mascot of the Second Canadian Infantry Brigade, and she attended her post with vigor. One day, Harry came running while she was doing her exercises in the tent. "You'll bring the whole place down!" he said with a laugh. She *had* grown.

It was winter when the order came:
The time had come to fight. Winnie
posed proudly with the men for pictures
to send home to their families.

Harry thought for a long time. His
head argued one way and then the other.
But his heart made up his mind.

He went to Winnie and said in a
serious way, "There's somewhere we
need to go." Winnie brushed the mud
off her nose and nuzzled in close.

Harry drove all the way to the Big City.

"Here we are," said Harry. "The London Zoo."

Harry took a deep breath. "Winnie, this is going to be your home for a while," he said. She tilted her head.

"We're shipping out to France," he explained. "I have to take care of the horses at the front."

She rested her big head against him.

"I know you want to come, but it's not safe."

Winnie's head bowed. Harry's hands were warm as sunshine, as usual.

"There is something you must always remember," Harry said. "It's the most important thing, really. Even if we're apart, I'll always love you. You'll always be my Bear."

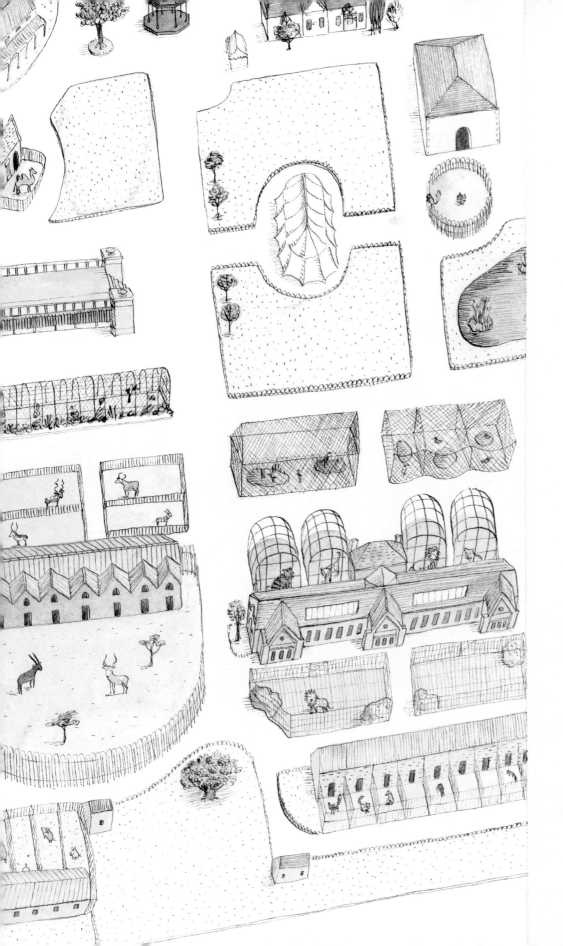

"Is that the end?"

"That's the end of Harry and Winnie's story," I said.

"But I don't want it to be over," said Cole.

"Sometimes," I said, "you have to let one story end so the next one can begin."

"How do you know when that will happen?"

"You don't," I said. "Which is why you should always carry on."

Once upon a time, there was a little boy with a stuffed Bear. He'd had his Bear ever since he was a baby. But somehow, the boy had never found the right name for him: He'd tried Teddy, and Edward, and even Big Bear.

One day, the boy went to visit
the London Zoo with his father,
and there was a bear—a *real* Bear—
on the Terraces there. Right away,
the boy thought, "There is something
special about that Bear." Her name
was Winnie.

They became true friends. The boy
was allowed to come right inside her
enclosure to play.

Once the boy had found Winnie,
he knew just what to call his stuffed
Bear. He named it Winnie-the-Pooh.

And the boy was called—

"Cole?" said Cole.

His name was Christopher Robin Milne. Christopher Robin would visit Winnie at the zoo, and then he would take his stuffed animal on all sorts of adventures in the wood behind his home.

His father, Alan Alexander Milne, wrote books all about them.

Harry's Winnie became Winnie-the-Pooh—and there has never been a more beloved bear.

"But what about Harry?" Cole asked.

When Harry visited Winnie at the zoo, he saw how happy she was. She was being raised. She was truly *loved*. And that was all he had ever wanted, from the moment they met at the train station in White River.

So, after the war, Harry returned to Winnipeg and his life as an animal doctor.

Before long, he was married and had a son named Fred, and Fred had a daughter named Laureen, and Laureen had a daughter named Lindsay.

Which is me.

And then *I* had a son.

When I saw you, I thought, "There is something special about this Boy." So I named you after your great-great-grandfather: Captain Harry Colebourn.

I named you Cole.

"That's me?" said Cole in a whisper.

"That's you."

"And that's Winnie?"

"Yes," I said. "That's Winnie."

"And it's all true?"

"Sometimes the best stories are," I said.

Cole's eyes grew big, and he said nothing for a long time.
Then he hugged his own bear close and let out a yawn that
reached far away, and they both turned over and fell asleep.

Harry as a young soldier

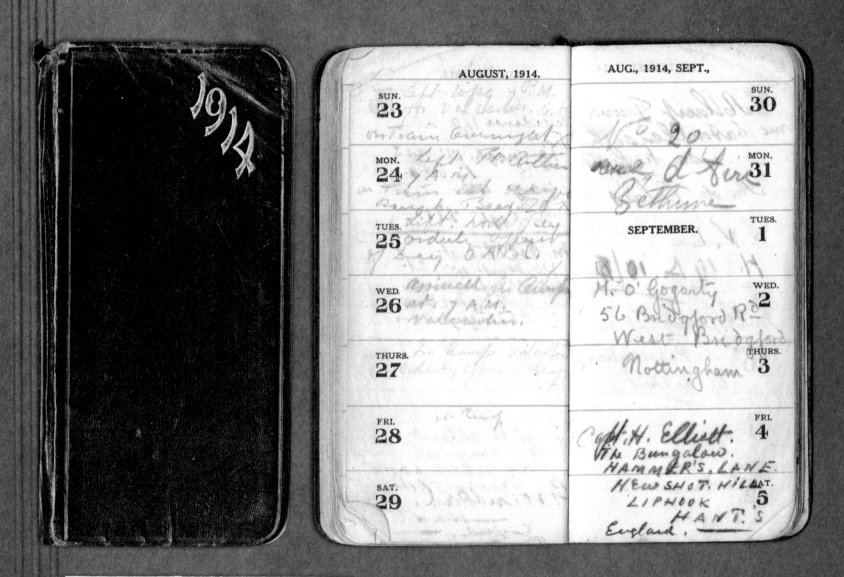

Harry kept diaries throughout World War I. This was the diary from 1914, the first year of the war.

The diary page from the day Harry found Winnie. On August 24, 1914, he wrote, "Bought bear $20."

Three soldiers with Winnie-at her post!

Winnie and Harry have what appears to be a laugh-and a snack.

Harry and his fellow soldiers with their Mascot, Winnie

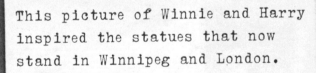
This picture of Winnie and Harry inspired the statues that now stand in Winnipeg and London.

The statue in Winnipeg was unveiled in 1992.

This photo was taken of
Winnie and Christopher
Robin in 1925 at the zoo
after they became friends.
Christopher Robin's father,
A. A. Milne, watches them
play from above.

This official Animal
Record Card shows that
Winnie began her stay at
the London Zoo on
December 9, 1914.

No. 1   Mappin Terrace HOUSE.
Winnie
American NAME. Black Bear   SEX. ♀
Ursus americanus
HABITAT.
White River. Ontario Dec. 1. 1919.
HOW ACQUIRED. Pres.ᵈ by Capt. Harry Coleborne. C.A.V.C. 7.3ˢ.
Depos.ᵈ by the 2ⁿᵈ Infantry Brigade
DATE OF ARRIVAL. Canadian Contingent
Dec. 9. 1914   METHOD & DATE OF DEPARTURE.
Died 12. 5. 34.
32,382.
(97—1000—4-19—W. & S.)